ROLLING STONES·40X20

BILLBOARD BOOKS *an imprint of*

Watson-Guptill Publications

NEW YORK

Produced by

INSIGHT EDITIONS

1299 4th St. Suite 305, San Rafael, CA 94901
www.insighteditions.com

First published in 2002 by Billboard Books,
An imprint of Watson-Guptill Publications,
A division of VNU Business Media, Inc.
770 Broadway
New York, NY 10003
www.watsonguptill.com

Library of Congress Cataloging-in-Publication Data
Library of Congress Card number: 2002109283

ISBN: 0-8230-8416-7

Printed in China
Designed and Printed by Palace Press International
www.palacepress.com
Front cover photo by Michael Cooper

First printing, 2002

1 2 3 4 5 6 7 8 9 / 10 09 08 07 06 05 04 03 02

ROLLING STONES · 40X20

BILLBOARD BOOKS

an imprint of
Watson-Guptill Publications

NEW YORK

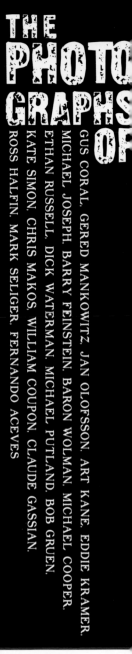

THE PHOTO GRAPHS OF

GUS CORAL. GERED MANKOWITZ. JAN OLOFSSON. ART KANE. EDDIE KRAMER. MICHAEL JOSEPH. BARRY FEINSTEIN. BARON WOLMAN. MICHAEL COOPER. ETHAN RUSSELL. DICK WATERMAN. MICHAEL PUTLAND. BOB GRUEN. KATE SIMON. CHRIS MAKOS. WILLIAM COUPON. CLAUDE GASSIAN. ROSS HALFIN. MARK SELIGER. FERNANDO ACEVES

EDITED BY
Chris Murray
with foreword by
Richard Harrington
text by the
photographers

This book is published in conjunction
with the exhibition

ROLLING STONES 40X20

A Fortieth-Anniversary Exhibition

GOVINDA GALLERY
1227 Thirty-fourth Street, N.W.
Washington, D.C. 20007
popart@govindagallery.com

A CKNOWLEDGMENT S

A heartfelt thanks to all of the photographers in this book and exhibition. Their images, like the Stones themselves, will endure. I am grateful to my editorial staff, Gabby Fisher and Carol Huh, at Govinda Gallery, as well as to Liz Murdock for her help transcribing the text. My thanks to everyone at Palace Press, especially Raoul and Gordon Goff. Thanks to my friend Jim Morrissey who went to that first Stones concert in New York City with me, to Tom Beach for our trip to Atlanta and to Chuck Rendelman for the show in Las Vegas. And most of all, thanks to the *Rolling Stones* who rock my world.

— Chris Murray,
Govinda Gallery

As the quintessential rock'n'roll band, the **Rolling Stones** have embraced, defied, twisted—and ultimately embodied—every imaginable rock and roll cliche and stereotype. They probably could have done it without making a sound.

Witness this silent book, which is nonetheless loud, rambunctious, chaotic, flamboyant, dangerous—all qualities attached to the Stones' music, and to their lives, but just as appropriate to their look. Like their music, the **Rolling Stones'** style is audacious and electrifying. To see them is to hear them.

Little wonder that photographers have always loved them: **Rolling Stones** pictures come with implied soundtracks. That's true even of the relatively airy innocence of the early days—so many days ago, forty years' worth now—when everything seemed as possible as it should have been impossible, before the Stones' single-minded devotion to gritty American blues, rock and rhythm 'n' blues led to the discovery of their own distinctive voices. Which led to the hysteria of the turbulent '60s and those perpetually rumbling undercurrents of danger—as much to the Stones themselves as to the culture of the times. After that, the gargantuan operatic concert forays of the '70s and '80s, and the glamorous ennui of men of wealth and curious tastes living in exile.

They were decadent dandies transformed into rock 'n' roll highwaymen, iconoclasts who became icons. With the tragic exception of co-founder Brian Jones—perhaps the most gifted, curious, provocative and fashionable Stone, he flamed out quickly—the band managed to outlast its contemporaries and outlive most of its addictions. They began calling themselves "The World's Greatest Rock & Roll Band" in the late '60s, and have reclaimed the title every decade since. How intriguing that their first American hit was a cover of Buddy Holly's "Not Fade Away," their first Top 10 a cover of Irma Thomas' "Time Is On My Side." Time has indeed stayed on their side and the images have refused to fade away.

And what glorious subjects they have been, particularly Mick Jagger, rock and roll's most famous hybrid—half rooster, half satyr—and always the center of attention with his feral physique, liquid hips and pouty lips. In sex, drugs and rock'n'roll, Jagger was the sex; glimmer, sometimes grimmer, twin Keith Richards the drugs. Rock 'n' roll was the combustible consequence of their partnership, and almost every picture tells the story of a relationship as unsinkable as it is unstable.

As photo subjects, Bill Wyman and Charlie Watts are like their bass playing and drumming: solid, immutable, dependable presences. The guitarists—the doomed Jones, the unconvinced Mick Taylor, the inevitable Ron Wood—are crucial, but never central. Even in the increasingly self-contained world of the *Rolling Stones*, it's Jagger and Richards who command the camera's eye to themselves.

Photographs can lie, but these don't. Some are pure documentary gold. Some were done with publicity clearly in mind, and some were unconscious propaganda; when you sense that eyes and lenses are always on you, you slip into poses and attitudes without necessarily being aware of it. For the most part, the *Rolling Stones* were perpetually self-aware—any kind of royalty requires the assumption of more than crowns. But they also knew who to trust, who to be unguarded with.

Which leads to this particular accumulation of historic images by many of the very best chroniclers of the *Rolling Stones* phenomena. Turn the pages and listen...

— Richard Harrington

P R E F A C E

I had the good fortune of attending the Rolling Stones' first concert in New York City. It was June 20, 1964, and the Stones were playing afternoon and evening gigs at Carnegie Hall. I went to the afternoon show and the **Stones** blew my mind.

I was a junior in high school in Manhattan at the time. A friend of mine and I had started going to the Saturday afternoon concerts at Carnegie Hall. My initiation into live music came with a truly amazing show by Ray Charles and his orchestra. We continued to go to the Carnegie Hall concerts and saw the Beach Boys and the Dave Clark Five. While leaving one of those concerts, a small card was handed out with a photo on it of the most unusual-looking band I had ever seen. The card read, "England's newest sensation, The **Rolling Stones.**" We had never heard of them. It was the next show at Carnegie Hall and we decided to go.

Nearly forty years have passed, but I will never forget the incredible buzz from that concert. It changed everything for me. The set that night included "Not Fade Away," "Walking the Dog," "Route 66," and "I Just Wanna Make Love to You," among others. I had not seen or heard anything like it since Elvis. The so-called "English Invasion" was on, but this was the first English band I saw that took American blues and R&B to rock and roll.

Mick Jagger's dancing and singing were hot! Brian Jones' charisma was so strong he seemed to front the band. Keith was the root of it all musically, and Bill and Charlie were rock steady. And the Stones made all the girls scream.

Four decades later, the **Rolling Stones** are still rolling. No other musical group has continued to endure like the **Rolling Stones.** The photographers in this book have documented many of the highlights from their amazing journey. Not only have the **Rolling Stones** given us some of the best rock and roll music, but they have also given us a lot to look at. This book is a 'tip-of-the-hat' to the greatest rock and roll band in the world.

– Chris Murray

Gus
CORAL

Photographing the Stones came by way of two friends of mine, Dick Fontaine, a documentary filmmaker, and James Miller, a graphic designer. We hung out together at the time. Dick was doing a five-minute spot in a half-hour program called *Tempo*, so we put our heads together to come up with the next big band. After talking to several people, the name *"The Rolling Stones"* came up. The next thing we heard is that they're doing a tour, and if we were quick we could catch up with them in Cardiff. So on the spur of the moment, Dick and I went to Cardiff and I took these photos.

At the concert in Cardiff, I was right in the wings of the stage. I had access. They didn't even think about security in those days. They didn't have minders and people to keep you out of certain areas. I was just there and the camera had a clear path. The big thing (and I didn't catch all of it) was the discussion about whether or not they would wear those houndstooth jackets. They almost didn't, and then decided they would. They preferred their street clothes, which were smarter in a casual kind of way.

After the concert, the *Stones* told us that they would be recording in the next couple of weeks and invited us to the EMI studios in Holborn. In the taxi shot, Holborn station is in the background. They were trying to get the cab fare together, you know, "Who's got five shillings?" or whatever. I was waiting for them at the door.

There was a different feel to the *Stones* in the studio shots compared to the stage shots. In the studio, they were surprisingly professional for a young band and just got on the job without a great deal of larking—they just played the music. Mick definitely had a charisma that was immediately apparent. Brian was very vain (though not so much to me) and very particular about his appearance. I can remember his vanity and I think that shows in some of the photos. I kind of warmed up to Charlie but it was hard because he is a very quiet, internal character...but I'm a bit like that as well. I thought he, rather than the others, was someone I could get along with personally. Keith was quiet, but so were the others. It was quite a subdued session. They were being serious about the music and getting the recording done.

I was a full-time, busy photographer then. I would photograph someone the day before and someone else the day after. Just another gig done for hire, mainly through word of mouth. But my work with the *Stones* in 1963 was close to my heart.

1963, BRIAN JONES AND MICK JAGGER. CARDIFF

1963, BILL WYMAN. KEITH RICHARDS
AND BRIAN JONES.
DE LANE LEA STUDIOS.
LONDON

1963, KEITH RICHARDS, MICK JAGGER, BRIAN JONES, CHARLIE WATTS AND BILL WYMAN,
OUTSIDE DE LANE LEA STUDIOS, LONDON

1963, KEITH RICHARDS, MICK JAGGER, BRIAN JONES AND BILL WYMAN, PAYING CAB
OUTSIDE OF DE LANE LEA STUDIOS, LONDON

1963, KEITH RICHARDS
AND BRIAN JONES, TUNING
UP, DE LANE LEA STUDIOS,
LONDON

1963, BILL WYMAN, BRIAN JONES AND MICK JAGGER.
CARDIFF

1963, CHARLIE WATTS. DE LANE LEA STUDIOS. LONDON

I was working with Chad and Jeremy,

an English duo who were a sort of folk-pop British version of the Everly Brothers, and they were appearing on a television show in 1964. Also on the show was Marianne Faithful, who had just released "As Tears Go By." Chad and Jeremy brought Marianne back to London and I joined the three of them for dinner. Instantly, I fell under Marianne's spell. She was bright and gorgeous, so I began photographing her within a few days. Her manager, Andrew Loog Oldham, who also managed the *Stones,* loved my pictures of Marianne and asked me to work with the Stones.

I had met Brian socially around the end of 1964, and I met all of them at Andrew's office once he had decided he wanted me to do a shoot. The first session I did with the Stones was in early 1965 at my studio in Mason's Yard. I took them out of the studio and into an adjacent space called Ormond Yard, where I photographed them. From that session came the cover of *Out of Our Heads*, or *December's Children* as it was called in America. We had a fantastic time, very laid back and informal. There were no publicists, stylists, or security; not even a roadie. It was just me and the guys. It was immensely exciting because they weren't the superstars they are today, but still, they were huge. "Satisfaction" was number one or about to be. Up until then, I'd been working with small acts with small labels, so the *Stones* was a massive leap for my career and incredibly exciting.

In the summer of that year, I got a call to say I was going to go on the tour. It was fantastic. I spent November and December in America on this extraordinary tour that covered forty-eight cities in sixty days. I was on stage with them every night. We ended up in Hollywood at RCA studios when "Get Off of My Cloud" was number one, and they were recording *Aftermath*. It was just a phenomenal whirlwind year for me, and for them, it was an extraordinary experience.

Throughout 1966, we did stuff around the UK, recording at Olympic Studios in Barnes in West London, and during home sessions with each of them as well as the Primrose Hill *Between the Buttons* photographs after an all night recording session. It was most interesting at the beginning. Brian had the most-evolved image, a defined and refined charisma. Mick and Keith were a bit raggedy. There was a little bit of money by the end of 1965, but it didn't start coming through until 1966, when they got the cars and the houses. When I first met the *Stones,* there was a very exciting, youthful energy. Every single was a new adventure; every album was "My God, we got away with it. What's next?" They were having a great time, and were working harder than any of them had been prepared for. Brian was still at the forefront of the band and really shared the spotlight with Mick in terms of fan worship and fanaticism. If you look at the pictures from 1965, the evolution of Keith's image is obvious from the beginning to the end of the year; you see him in those cool shades, the leather jacket with the sheepskin collar, and the big Gibson Hummingbird guitar at RCA. Brian is just beginning to show signs of strain. Those pictures were taken less than a year after Ormond Yard.

Gered
MANKOWITZ

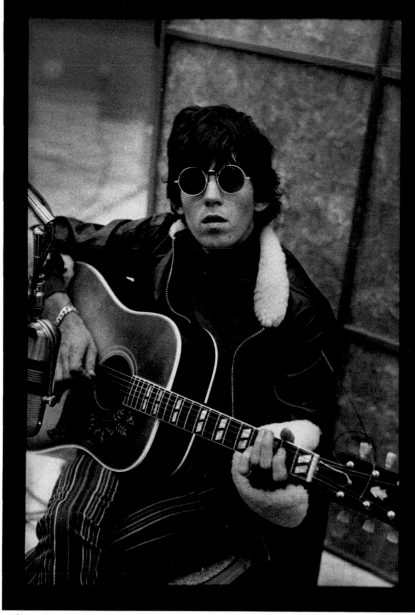

12/50

The Palladium in New York was raw and exciting. "Satisfaction" was their biggest hit yet and "Get Off of My Cloud'" was zooming up the charts. When they ended the show with "Get Off of My Cloud" the buzz was just fantastic. I can't hear that today without feeling that same feeling. Shooting at the Palladium and other shows felt very natural because they were at ease with me walking around during the shows. The vibration, both physical and emotional, was immense. You felt the music through your feet and you felt the extraordinary power of the kids who were just screaming and loving it. Sure enough some girl would break through, leap on stage, and wrap herself around Brian before anybody knew it. A pile of palpitating teenagers would be in the back. Mick just manipulated the audience into an absolute frenzy night after night. The whole experience was electric.

They would rush off the stage and would be at the airport before anyone realized the show was over. I was so inexperienced and amateurish in the way I managed everything. I didn't run around with my camera around my neck. I had a little metal camera case, and a couple of Nikon lenses, and I had to get all my stuff packed and in the limo quickly, in danger of being left behind. I didn't take pictures after the shows; we'd get on the plane, have dinner, arrive at three o'clock in the morning and be whisked to our hotel in some other God-forsaken place—like Raleigh, North Carolina—or in some dead city sitting there with no girls, no drugs, and no place open to get booze. It was a bizarre but fantastic, and educational, routine that changed my career.

Then there was 1967. I shot the *Satanic Majesties* recording session, but the relationship between Andrew and the band and, consequently, me and the band, started falling apart, along with Brian. It was a very difficult and strange time.

According to my deal with Andrew, I was paid for every picture I took. Although the **Stones** bought an individual picture from me since I had the copyrights, none of it really got used at that time. In the last few years, they acknowledged and published my pictures because they were taken at the peak of their initial success, at the start of an amazing forty years. "Satisfaction" and "Get Off of My Cloud" were brilliant rock songs, and everything was right. Brian was still a really active, important contributing member of the **Stones.** In terms of the initial energy, 1965-66 was a fantastic vintage. How lucky was I to be around for that moment, that period?

19/150 1966, MICK JAGGER WITH ASTON MARTIN,
LONDON

5/50

19/150

1966, *BETWEEN THE BUTTONS. PRIMROSE HILL. LONDON*

1965, THE ROLLING STONES. AMERICA

The Stones photographs were taken on the set of a TV show called Ready Steady Go with a live audience in Wembley. I was writing a monthly column for a Swedish magazine to earn some money and I used to go there regularly. I wasn't really aware at the time of trying to take a great shot. It was all done on my own and without flash, only with available lighting. I made three pounds and three shillings for a picture in a magazine, which was great.

When the *Rolling Stones* came along, they were exciting. I used to meet them in all the various clubs where John Lennon and the Beatles and everybody used to go, such as Scotch of Saint James, The Speakeasy, and The Revolution. If you were hanging around the pub scene in London at that time, you got to meet all the bands. Ian Stewart was on the scene with the *Stones* and did a little bit of playing here and there. Brian Jones and I used to go out drinking together. The first Indian meal I ever had was with Brian and Viv Prince on King's Road. Viv was the drummer of The Pretty Things and, to be honest, the *Stones* were quite influenced by The Pretty Things.

Ever since then, I've enjoyed the *Stones* and they've always put out good records. But I must say my favorite *Stones* music came from the period with Brian Jones and his 'sitar'...that was the real *Stones* sound. He also played the vibraphone and percussion instruments. The band had that Bo Diddley and Buddy Holly sound going, too.

The *Stones,* the Beatles and many of the other bands later became superstars, but in those days they weren't. Even though they were still accessible, we never took cameras into the clubs. Unlike today, where some photographers hide to take scandalous shots of someone and make a lot of money, in those days we had respect for the musicians, and we got respect from them. There was no money involved...we'd be happy to get a couple of sandwiches and a pint.

Jan
OLOFFSON

1966, MICK JAGGER AND KEITH RICHARDS. READY STEADY GO, WEMBLEY

1966, BRIAN JONES AND MICK JAGGER. READY STEADY GO. WEMBLEY

1966, MICK JAGGER.
READY STEADY GO, WEMBLEY

1966, KEITH RICHARDS. BRIAN JONES AND IAN STEWART. READY STEADY GO. WEMBLEY

Art
K A N E

**P*erformance shots are
a waste of time;*** they look like
everyone else's. If you want to shoot a band like the
Rolling Stones, then grab them, own them, and
twist them into what you want to say about them.

Photographing Mick Jagger, I realized that photography isn't merely an act of selection, but is equally an act of rejection, deciding what you won't allow in.

When one thinks of a portrait, one thinks of a face. A permanent record. A vicarious approach to immortality. I always felt that presenting faces was never quite enough. I wanted to communicate the unseen elements in a personality like Brian Jones.

1966, BRIAN JONES.
PHOTO SHOOT FOR
MCCALL'S MAGAZINE, LONDON

1966, KEITH RICHARDS.
PHOTO SHOOT FOR
MCCALL'S MAGAZINE, LONDON

BRIAN JONES 1966

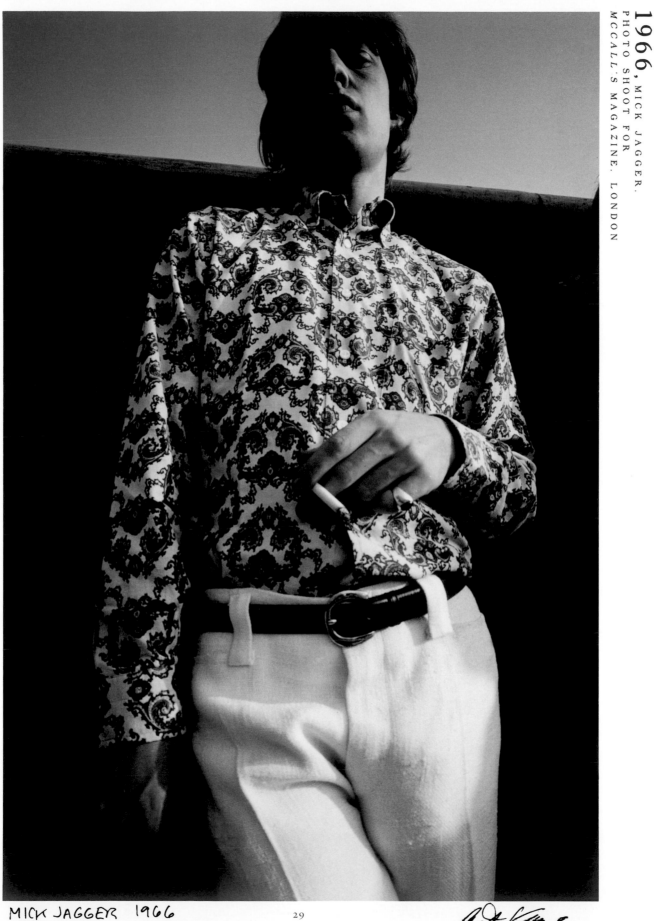

MICK JAGGER 1966

I photographed the Stones while working in the studio as an engineer from 1967 to 1968. Jimmy Miller was the first American producer to come over to England to work with Chris Blackwell's label, Island Records. Because of Jimmy's success with Traffic, which he and I produced together, the *Stones* approached him and, of course, he jumped at it. Jimmy was the producer for *Beggars Banquet* and I was his engineer.

Previously, when I worked with the *Stones* as an assistant with Glynn Johns, I couldn't take pictures, but as a senior engineer I could. I used to keep a camera on the console, sitting right next to me, loaded and ready to go. I'd snap pictures behind me, or run into the studio, shoot, and run back into the control room. My main function was engineering, but the camera was always there with me. I couldn't use the flash. Sometimes musicians would joke, "Kramer, get the fuck out of my face, you bastard." The bands got used to my being there with the camera and just ignored me. It became part of the furniture. My left hand would be on the console, my right hand would hold the camera and I'd just swing around in my chair, click with one hand, swing back, and keep working.

I also did some live recording for them in Cleveland and some other places. I remember going on stage just before the show in Cleveland and tuning up Charlie's drums. He said, "Hey I never tune up my drums!" and I replied, "Yeah, I can tell." Ian Stewart was an absolutely unflappable guy and a wonderful keyboard player. He was their roadie, and drove them around in a VW bus when they first started. They used to hide him on stage.

Brian was the unsung hero of the *Stones,* and the most creative. He would take chances with different instruments and musical cultures and try to incorporate them into the *Stones'* music. He was a great guy, and a very close friend of Jimi Hendrix. Brian absolutely revered Jimi, and Jimi really liked him. I love my photographs of Brian with his head back and the light shining. He looks almost angelic.

On November 27, 1969, Jimi's birthday, I photographed the *Stones* at Madison Square Garden. Jimi said, "Come with me, let's go up and hang out at the Garden." We went backstage and Jimi sat down with Mick, Charlie, and Ian. How could you resist taking that picture?

Eddie KRAMER

1967, BRIAN JONES, OLYMPIC STUDIOS, LONDON

1969, KEITH RICHARDS, MADISON SQUARE GARDEN, NEW YORK

1969, JIMI HENDRIX AND MICK JAGGER. MADISON SQUARE GARDEN. NEW YORK

Michael JOSEPH

I had just survived a few months in Vietnam covering the war for Town (England's answer to *Esquire*) and had shot numerous White Horse Whiskey ads. The latter taught me the trick of handling animals by using a megaphone to create unusual sounds. This helped me coordinate a hungry goat, a dopey sheep, two dogs (one stuffed), and a cat, in addition to the semi-stoned *Stones* at eleven a.m. in a Victorian Society Painters Studio in Hampstead, London.

The location was a medieval jousting pavilion, which was a great backdrop with the help of many smoke bombs. Afterward, the *Stones* changed into cricket gear for the back cover image, with a two-legged piano as an added prop.

Handling the *Stones* was easier than the animals. They were all in a state of shock from a police raid on Brian Jones' flat the day before...and the megaphone is mightier than the sword. Keith was the most cooperative, so my image of Keith and the Boston Terrier with Mick leering in the background is my favorite image.

The assignment was to shoot on 10 x 8 color, which is slow to record and notoriously difficult to realize depth of field. As a safety, I shot a couple of rolls of Ektrachrome 200 and some black & white film on a Hasselblad super-wide, which I developed and printed overnight. I wanted to show Mick my Kodalith prints so that they would sign some for me. During a tea break in Chester (Derbyshire), I presented some color prints, as well as the Kodalith prints. Mick was knocked out by the richness and depth of the Kodaliths and he immediately signed and dedicated the portrait to me—my unique trophy from a momentous shoot.

Mick was so delighted with the Kodaliths he decided to elbow the color. Luckily, some were used for the American sleeve. He had the orgy scene hand-colored, which gave the provocative image an even more bizarre, Bunuel-ish look.

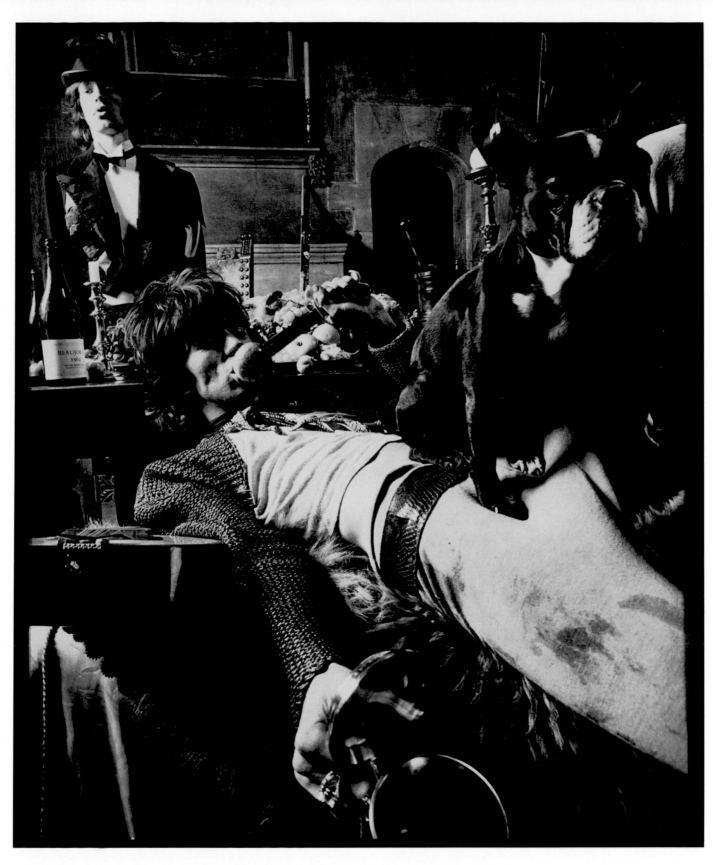

Mick, Keith & Roy after the "Rolling Stones" "Beggars Banquet" — London 1968

Michael Joseph   7/250
Iris Kodalith

1968, THE ROLLING STONES PLAYING CRICKET, CHESHIRE PARK

1968, MICK JAGGER, LONDON

Mick called and said, "We have something called Beggars Banquet,"

and he asked us to do the photos. Tom Brooks and I agreed to do it. I went over to my Porsche mechanic on Cahuenga Boulevard because I remembered that he had a funky fucking bathroom. I said, "Let's put the **Rolling Stones** on the wall." Mick and Keith came over and we put all kinds of shit on the walls, right in Hollywood. Tom wrote on there; my name's on there. I also wrote a poem to my wife. If you look really carefully, you'll see a cock with two balls.

Barry
FEINSTEIN

That created a controversy. One of the directors wouldn't put the album out when they saw it and held it up for six months. It was published in *Time* and was supposed to be the cover for the whole thing, but they did the white LP instead. Years later when they put the CD out, they used our shots for the front and back covers.

I know we were having fun, how could we not? That's just how it works. Allen Kline was managing them. *I don't think I ever got paid for those shots.*

Baron
WOLMAN

The first shots I did of the Stones were of Mick on the set of the film Performance in 1968, when I was the chief photographer for *Rolling Stone* magazine. The shoot took place in the studio in London and, as you can see, Mick was very heavily made up. I love that photo; it was an incredibly memorable time. That same week, I shot George Harrison at Apple and the Who recording *Tommy*.

I took my first live shots of the Stones in 1969 at the Oakland Coliseum. I was so excited that I wasn't checking my equipment all the time and my lens wasn't locked into the camera. Many of the shots were out of focus. For the show in 1978, I was the only photographer allowed on stage because I was close to Bill Graham, the producer of that show. I shot from in front of and behind the stage. I had access, the kind you wouldn't see now. That's the reason I got out of rock and roll photography. The late 1970s was the last time responsible and professional photographers had the freedom to get the great shots. Now, once you get all of the security clearances, you have to sign away your firstborn just to get the shoot, not even to get on stage. Rock and roll photographers have been relegated to slave labor, the third-class citizen. When access is denied or limited, it's like having your balls cut off. You become a photographer-eunuch.

The *Stones* are the ultimate rock and roll band. Every time you go to a show you get so energized you have to dance right in your seat.

1969, MICK JAGGER. OAKLAND

Michael
COOPER
Text by his son, Adam Cooper

Michael came to shoot the Stones through their mutual friend Robert Fraser. Dad hit it off with the band, and became particularly close friends with Keith. The rest is history.

For the *Satanic Majesties* cover, the **Stones** came up with the idea of producing these acrylic movable discs so that the heads of the band members moved depending on how you angled the album cover itself. The only place in the world that could do that was a studio in New York. They went off to New York and that's why you have those shots of the band outside buying all the clothing and the stuff to build the set. Those images are still amazing. Can you imagine Mick Jagger going out there now and sticking things on the set and building the whole thing himself? They shot that session there and the result was incredible. I think it was Allen Kline who got the bill estimating the cost to mass distribute this new effect and he threw it straight out the window. He said, "Forget it, it's just going to cost too much." Production of the special cover was limited to the first five hundred or so, and the rest were just a straight print run of the image itself. I still have an album cover with the plastic acrylic and the moving heads.

During the '60s, Michael and Keith were great buddies. Lots of people said they used to look like each other, so it was like the terrible twins on King's Road everyday. They really hit it off for all the good reasons...and all the wrong reasons.

In the early days, Michael was working principally through *Vogue*. Back then, you were told what to shoot, where to shoot, how many rolls to shoot, and when to deliver the work. Michael got very frustrated with the restrictions of fashion photography. That's why he got out of it as quickly as possible, and that's why he enjoyed shooting the **Stones**. The images make absolutely clear that Michael's stuff is really 'fly on the wall.' It's not constructed and the light is entirely natural. The strength of his work lies in great composition and grabbing the moment when it happens, which is really difficult to do. You have a second to do it, and if you ask the subject to do it again, the effort becomes posed. The *Satanic Majesties* and *Sergeant Pepper* covers were about a group of buddies sitting around and coming up with this really weird and wonderful idea. I know Michael would be extremely proud today of having done the *Satanic Majesties* and *Sergeant Pepper* covers.

Michael's talent came from an obsession for photography and living with the camera twenty-four hours a day. No matter what state he was in, he managed to find himself at the right place at the right time to capture magnificent images.

1966, "PINTA POSTER."
MICK JAGGER AND KEITH
RICHARDS, LONDON

1968, KEITH RICHARDS. JOSHUA TREE. CALIFORNIA

1966, BRIAN JONES RECORDING AT
OLYMPIC STUDIOS, LONDON

1969, MICK JAGGER, HYDE PARK, LONDON

1967, KEITH RICHARDS AND BRIAN JONES.
SATANIC MAJESTIES PHOTO SESSION, NEW YORK

In 1968, at the age of *22, I was a young American with a Nikon living in London,* working as a volunteer with autistic children, and trying to be a writer. I left America on a European vacation, but I had my eye on England. When I first arrived, I knew no one. I was already a huge fan of British music, and everything that was known in America as the "British Invasion." I discovered the Who after I arrived in England, but the Beatles and the *Rolling Stones* were already legendary.

The first time I saw the *Rolling Stones* became one of those permanent memories, like knowing exactly where you were when Kennedy was shot or when man walked on the moon. I was looking at a Gered Mankowitz photograph, of course. I still think Gered took the defining images of the *Stones* and his work is the most memorable for me, especially *December's Children, 12 x 5,* and *Between the Buttons.*

The look of the *Stones* helped make them exciting, as much as their music. When I came to photograph them, the pictures I took were quite different from Gered's group shots. More often than not I shot them individually, more like an outside observer, catching them in moments. There's a value in these candid shots that is so rare in today's world where packaging and marketing predominate. The photographs can give a sense that, as great as the "stars" are and as momentous as the music, the gig, or the legend may be, it's still really made by humans.

But all of that is in hindsight. At the time, I lived in a one-room flat in sleepy London town and loved it, though not simply for the rock and roll of it, which seemed remarkably hidden. Then, one day, a college friend arrived from America. In turn, he invited one of his friends, Jonathan Cott, who was a some-time interviewer for this new American magazine, *Rolling Stone*. Jonathan—who saw a couple of the black and white photos I had taken, mostly of children—asked, "Do you want to photograph Mick Jagger?" This is partly why I still believe, as John Lennon said, "Life is what happens while you're making other plans."

I photographed Mick in their little office on Maddox Street while Jonathan interviewed him. The people in the *Stones'* office seemed to like the photographs when they saw them, and to like me, so I was asked to do it again. "I photographed the *Rolling Stones Rock and Roll Circus*, as well as the single sleeve for *Honky Tonk Woman* and the album cover for *Through the Past Darkly*. By this point, I had become sort of their unofficial, official photographer, and when I showed up in LA before their 1969 tour, I was asked to join. There were only thirteen of us, including the *Stones*, and we traveled on commercial airliners. It seemed very intimate by today's standards but, even then, Ian Stewart was complaining about how overblown it had all become. That tour ended in Altamont, and little was the same afterwards.

I worked with them again in 1972, also on tour. Much had changed. The primacy of music seemed to recede as the age of celebrity commenced. Whereas in 1969 the backstage visitors were the Beach Boys or Jimi Hendrix (and Abbie Hoffman in Chicago), in 1972 it was Truman Capote, Terry Southern, and Princess Lee Radziwell. There were many more photographers as well—Annie Liebovitz for *Rolling Stone*, and Jim Marshall for Life.

When the *Stones* roll around, I still go to the concerts with my friend Georgia Bergman, who ran the Stones' office from 1966 until after the 1972 tour. The venues are immense, the stage vast, and the technology integral. The showmanship of it remains staggering, and the rock and roll timeless.

Ethan
RUSSELL

1972, ROLLING STONES, US TOUR

1972, KEITH RICHARDS.
SEATTLE CUSTOMS

Dick
WATERMAN

T**he first date of the Stones' European tour in 1970* took place in Malmo, Sweden, a ferry ride across from Copenhagen. The show was scheduled to start around seven p.m. At around four thirty, this gigantic arena was entirely empty except for a couple of security guards and a couple of ushers. Chip Monk, the stage manager, intoned as what he would for every show: "LADIES AND GENTLEMEN, THE ***ROLLING STONES!" They ran on stage in a specific order and in single file so they didn't trip over each other. Bill was stationed at the farthest amplifier, so he came on stage first. He was followed by Keith going to his amp, Charlie to the drum riser, and then Mick Taylor to his amp. Mick Jagger would come up last, run to the front, and wave a top hat or a scarf to catch the audience's eye and give them something to look at during the five or ten seconds it took to plug in the two guitars and bass.

To an empty stadium, they did the opener, "Jumpin' Jack Flash." I noticed there was a rug on stage for Mick, so that as he spun and whirled and dipped backwards, he knew precisely where he was on the stage by the pattern of the rug. He knew how close he could come to the edge of the stage, so that grabbing hands couldn't get his ankles. They did the whole show—maybe seventy-five minutes—every song end to end. The crowd gathering in the parking lot could hear the music, and it started a frenzy outside. The *Stones* ran through the entire concert and musicians were pouring sweat with towels wrapped around their necks. As the last chord of the music faded out, Mick looked out over the empty seats and said, "OK, let 'em in."

By the time I met them in 1970, they were already veteran performers and certainly well-known. I began shooting them because Ahmet Ertegun at Atlantic Records and I had discussed signing Buddy Guy and Junior Wells. He called me to ask if Buddy and Junior together would open for the *Stones* in Europe, so I said, "Yeah, sure."

On tour, I was with them and the rest of the traveling crew and entourage day and night. I just melted into the background and they were comfortable with me on stage right away. They wouldn't turn around and say, "Who are you?" I was the guy who was friends with Buddy Guy and had a Buddy Guy/Junior Wells "All Access." I would be up on the edge of the stage.

Even though I had been photographing blues musicians and folk people in the 1960s, I wasn't into photography in a serious, professional manner. In fact, none of these photos of the *Stones* have ever been published before. I was carrying only one camera and one or two lenses. I wasn't using a huge thing, just a 135mm which, from a technical point of view, isn't a big zoom. But I had great access. Nowadays, artists want to protect their image for their egos and also for financial purposes. They want a hundred percent lock down and complete control over what photos get out. In recent years, I have had to clear it with management, agency, and venue to photograph people. Back in those days with the *Stones*, the photographer wasn't the enemy.

1970, KEITH RICHARDS. PARIS. FRANCE

1970, MICK JAGGER, OSLO, NORWAY

1970, THE ROLLING STONES. ROME. ITALY

1970, MICK TAYLOR AND KEITH RICHARDS. FRANKFURT, GERMANY

1970, MICK JAGGER, VIENNA, AUSTRIA

NYC '78

Aside from the fact that shooting the Stones was great for my career as a photographer, I've always loved the band. I've been watching the *Stones* live since 1964. I came out of that whole R&B/jazz thing that the *Stones* and everybody came out of. While I was living in the north-west part of London, which is the equivalent of Queens, I saw them on a packaged show with the Ronettes and the Everly Brothers. It was amazing.

In 1972, I had a studio with a friend who was bank-rolling me, but I couldn't get any work. I finally told him I was going to quit, get a job, and pay him back. We went out and got drunk. The next morning I went back to the studio to clear up my stuff when a phone call came from *Disc and Music Echo*, a pop magazine. Judy, the editor's

1978, BOB MARLEY, MICK JAGGER AND PETER TOSH, PALLADIUM THEATRE, NEW YORK

Michael PUTLAND

assistant, asked if I would do a shoot for them that day and I replied, "Actually, Judy, I'm quitting today. I'm giving up." "Well I think you might want to do this," she said. The assignment that saved my career was Mick...just out of the blue. After that, I began photographing everyone for that magazine every week. I shot him again on the train to Cardiff Castle in 1973. Then I did the European tour that same year.

They were all good-looking, photogenic guys in their own way. Charlie and, of course, Ronnie were brilliant and so was Mick Taylor when he was there. Obviously, Mick and Keith were fantastic to shoot. In all my contacts with Mick, in those days I found him a bit intimidating, although he's a very fair, terrific guy. Keith in those days was a little distant but he's always been great. And Bill—he'll kill me for saying this—maybe he wasn't the most photogenic but he had a booty sort of look. He was the one who got all the girls anyway.

Michael Putland

1978, KEITH RICHARDS AND MICK JAGGER, NEW YORK

1973, MICK JAGGER,
APOLLO, GLASGOW, SCOTLAND

1974, THE ROLLING STONES,
"IT'S ONLY ROCK AND ROLL" VIDEO,
LONDON

Bob

GRUEN

I was a huge Stones fan. In 1964 or 1965, I ran into a friend of mine on 14th Street who was scalping tickets for a concert. The *Stones* were the first band I ever saw in concert and it totally blew me away. Until then, I had seen bands only in bars. I saw them again in 1969 with Tina Turner. My first assignment to photograph them came in 1972 through Lisa Robinson, then editor of several magazines including Rock Scene. Over the years, I got to do some of the *Stones'* events around New York, including a lot of press conferences.

The photograph of Mick and Andy Warhol, who did the cover of the *Love You Live* album, was taken at Trax nightclub. They were signing autographs at a press event for the record release party. The band was very accessible that day, meeting with the press, going from one table to another talking to people, laughing it up, having drinks, and signing anything people brought with them. I think they had tablecloths that matched the record, and Mick was signing those too. Mick and Andy were obviously comfortable with each other and knew each other very well by then.

Mick's great because he's very expressive and moves a lot.

There isn't one pose and you've got the whole thing. He changes every second and you have to keep chasing him around the stage. He actually moves so fast it's hard to get a clear shot.

You can't take a bad picture of Keith. Keith is just so cool. With other people, the eyes are drooping or the mouth is slack, and you would never use it. But with him, every shot is killer because he is so charismatic. He was pretty drugged out in the '70s, but he seemed to be waking up in the '80s. By the time of his solo albums, we started to see another side to Keith. The concerts would start in the dark, and the band would come out and have a meditative moment before playing. Very often, he would drop to his knees as if to thank some spiritual guide for seeing him through. That photograph captures a more spiritual Keith, rather than the typical 'out of it' Keith.

When I shoot the *Stones,* I sing along as I do it, because I'm such a fan. But it's hard work and you have to stay alert because you get a photo pass for a few minutes only. You have to shoot so much film so fast. People ask what songs they did, but I don't remember. I'm just so busy shooting.

Looking at my pictures, they seem to talk to me and take me right back to being there. I can practically hear and smell those times. I like those memories. I had fun, and have fun looking back at it.

KEITH RICHARDS · NYC · 1993

NYC 97

ANDY WARHOL + MICK JAGGER - NYC - 1977

Kate
SIMON

1978, MICK JAGGER, RONNIE WOOD
AND KEITH RICHARDS, NEW YORK

In 1975, I was living in London and working as a staff photographer for *Sounds*, a weekly British music paper similar to *New Music Express* or *Melody Maker*. I shot concerts constantly, and I got an assignment to shoot the *Rolling Stones*, who were playing Earl's Court. I went on my own to shoot them in Vienna that same year, and then in New York in 1978, just because I felt like doing it.

As a photographer, my only frustration with photographing the *Stones* at Earl's Court was that Mick ran back and forth on the stage without stopping. I was a seasoned shooter, but to get a shot of him was a real challenge with all of his movement. But every once in a while you'd get him—you could tell when he was saying, "All right, I'm ready to give you the shot." He'd come right up to the lip of the stage and give you one. God help you if you didn't get it when he gave it to you.

The *Stones'* longevity is an indication of their artistic discipline. These men deserve a lot of respect. At the time, I definitely was a fan because I only shot things that I loved. Their shows were totally professional and they delivered the goods. They were tremendously exciting, unique, and masterful. They were brilliant showmen who took it very seriously. In my photographs from Earl's Court, Mick is clearly a man who took costuming extremely seriously... not to mention his physical shape. He just looks like a dancer. Keith Richards has so much class and such an amazing sense of style that there isn't anyone who even closely compares. He created the archetype.

I shot most of these images almost thirty years ago. When you return to some images after you've put them away and let then bake for twenty-five years, they look great. Something that you didn't see twenty-five years ago can look spectacular now.

1975, RONNIE WOOD AND
KEITH RICHARDS. LONDON

1975, MICK JAGGER AND KEITH RICHARDS.
LONDON

1975, MICK JAGGER. LONDON

1975, BILL WYMAN. RONNIE WOOD AND
MICK JAGGER. LONDON

Chris
MAKOS

These photos were taken in Montauk, Long Island.

I have no memory, so that's why I take pictures...to remind myself that I actually did things.

I had met Mick a year or so earlier in Paris, playing backgammon with one of the Guinness beer girls or something. We were on the Île de Paris with Fred Hughes [Andy Warhol's assistant] and all those people. Everybody was very chatty and it was cool.

The *Stones* had rented Andy Warhol and Paul Morrisey's house out on Montauk to rehearse for their 1982 North American tour. Andy must have been there, but I don't remember. They were rehearsing at the main house. I was just out there at the time and I said, "Can I take some pictures?" They said, "Sure," and Keith was holding a skull while the others stood around. It's too hard to get that many people together looking interesting, so I took separate pictures and pieced them together, much the way people would do today with PhotoShop and the computer.

They were all pretty cool and it shows in the photos. They had much fewer wrinkles than they do now.

1981, MICK JAGGER, MONTAUK, LONG ISLAND, NEW YORK

William
C O U P O N

I took these photographs for a cover of Rolling Stone magazine because Mick's album, She's the Boss, had just come out. The shoot was weeks in the making because we were waiting for Mick to make the call to say it was OK. I kept being put on hold, not knowing when it was going to happen. Meanwhile, I was asked to do the center for a *New York Times* Sunday Magazine cover story on Elie Weisel, so I spent the whole day shooting him in his house with his wife. At around five o'clock in the afternoon when I was just about wrapping up, I got a call from **Rolling Stone** saying, "Mick Jagger's at Charivari shopping and he's coming over to your place at seven thirty." I said, "You're kidding me, I'm just wrapping up a shoot here. I didn't know it was going to be that quick. OK, wow."

I got off the phone and said to Elie Weisel, "You won't believe this but I've got to go. I've got a shoot with Mick Jagger at my place." He replied, "Oh, who's Mick Jagger?" I went back home and did the shoot with Mick Jagger and at the end of it I said to him, "I had a shoot earlier with Elie Weisel," and he said, "Who's Elie Weisel?"

When I showed him my portfolio, Mick said, "So I see we're doing art here, are we?"

I asked him to put on my bathrobe because I liked the color on him. At the end, I asked him if he wanted to do anything else since I had done what I wanted. He said, "Well heck no, you've already got me in your dressing gown." At one point during the shoot, I went up to Mick Jagger and did, "I'm a monkey!" (I had been doing impressions of him since I was in college.) He just looked at me and said, "Oh my...uugh." The shoot took a while and he hung out at the house with me and my wife at the time. He had a couple of people with him, Laurie Kratochvil, Rolling Stone magazine's Director of Photography, and his stylist. Mick was easy to work with. He was Mr. Charming, really playing into the camera and making the whole shoot progress smoothly.

1983, MICK JAGGER. COVER OF *ROLLING STONE* MAGAZINE. NEW YORK

1983, MICK JAGGER.
ROLLING STONE
MAGAZINE PHOTO
SESSION. NEW YORK

1975, MICK JAGGER, MADISON SQUARE GARDEN, NEW YORK

Claude
GASSIAN

When I first began photograph-ing, my most successful shots were taken at the *Stones'* concerts in the early 1970s. As a novice, I found it easier to hide behind the lights and in the shadows of their overwhelmingly photogenic personalities. I crossed paths with each of them on several occasions throughout the '70s and '80s. The encounters were brief but always incredible and resulted in great images. Keith selected one of my photos, "Antwerpen 1973," for his first solo album, *Run Rudolph Run.* During the '90s, I spent much more time with them on tour and, consequently, had the opportunity to get more intimate, personal shots. These allowed me to express visually what I had experienced through their music.

Much time has passed, yet I still have the impression that the *Stones* haven't really changed. Looking back on my negatives, I relive those great live moments and the excitement I felt capturing them. The visual impact of the *Stones* that so obsessed me in the beginning still endures.

1990, KEITH RICHARDS AND MICK JAGGER, EN ROUTE
FROM MADRID, SPAIN, TO MARSEILLE, FRANCE

1985, MICK JAGGER, HOTEL
DE CRILLION, PARIS, FRANCE

1973, KEITH RICHARDS.
ANTWERPEN. HOLLAND

ROSS
HALFIN

This photograph of Keith was taken in a hotel corridor in Denmark in 1992 during Keith's "*Main Offender*" tour. I was quite surprised when he turned up, as he was early, but he was quite happy to wait while I finished setting up. I had fifteen minutes to do it. He couldn't have been more co-operative and helpful.

What can you say? It's Keith, the easiest subject there is to shoot. He's great every time.

2/50

Ross Hal...

1997, KEITH RICHARDS,
OKLAHOMA CITY

Mark
SELIGER

***D*uring a session for Rolling Stone magazine,** I was shooting individual portraits and, at the end, a group picture. Keith was sitting back, smoking a cigarette, and having a good time. My patience was running a little thin, as it was for everybody, so I said to him, "Keith we've got to take your picture." Keith replied, "Oh, I don't really want to do this, do you? I've been photographed with them for thirty fucking years, and it's fucking boring."

When doing publicity pictures for the *"Voodoo Lounge"* tour or shooting for **Rolling Stone,** I didn't expect them to be such generous and open guys. There wasn't an overwhelming sense of stardom or celebrity associated with their work. They're just really proud to be doing what they're doing, and to be doing it so well. They were extremely enthusiastic about the album and were playing it nonstop. It's like being at the end of a journey and reaping the rewards of your work.

As a youngster, I listened to a little bit of the **Stones,** but I got my first real taste when I was on a family trip. We stopped for lunch in a crappy little dive on Cape Cod and my brother walked up to a jukebox. The first song that came up was "Sympathy for the Devil" and I thought, "Wow, that sounds amazing!" My first concert was in Texas after the release of *"Some Girls"* and it was incredible. I was a late bloomer for the **Stones** but I loved them.

I have enormous respect for the **Stones.** Knowing that people can still put it out in such a big way and have a great time is infectious.

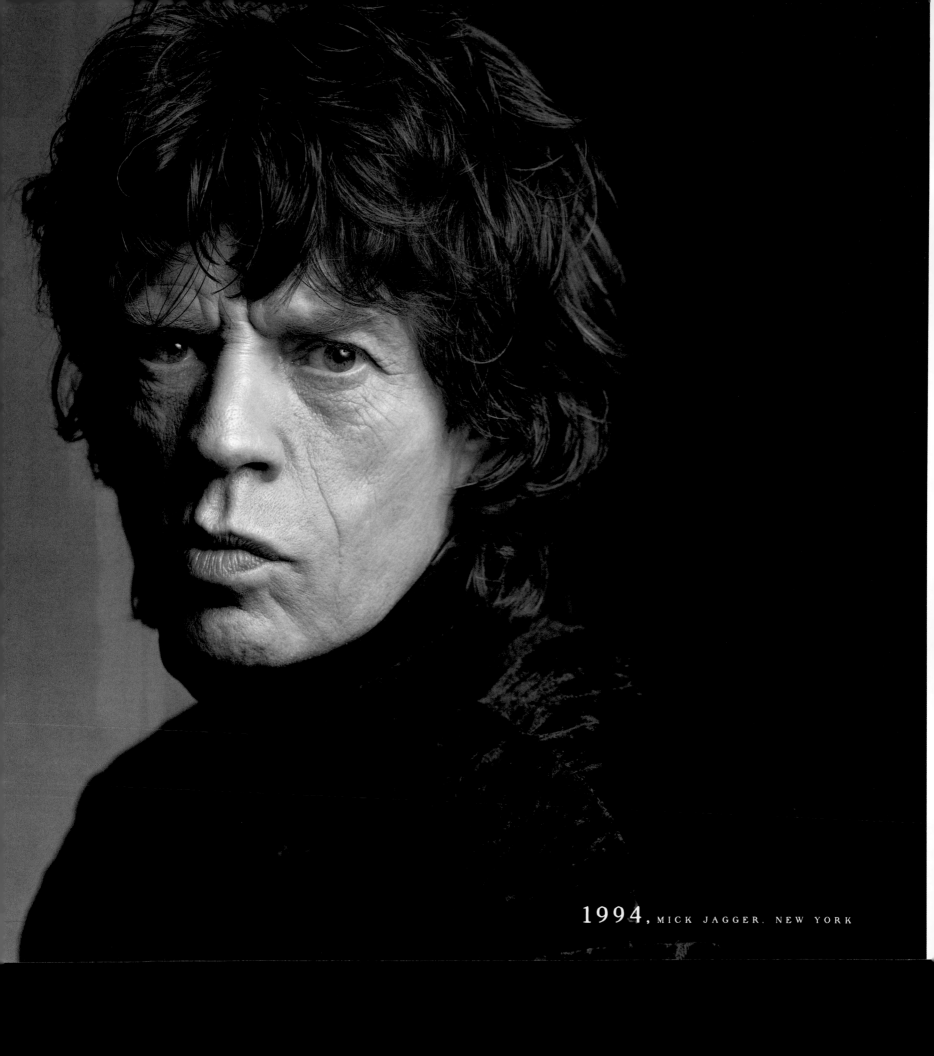

1994, MICK JAGGER, NEW YORK

1994,
KEITH RICHARDS,
NEW YORK

1995. THE ROLLING STONES. BROOKLYN. NEW YORK

*T*he very first time I photographed the Stones was in 1994 at Giant Stadium in New York. I was commissioned by a Mexican promoter, who was bringing the *Stones* the following year to Mexico City and wanted to have some advance photographs for the local press. After shooting the Woodstock festival that summer, I met the *Stones.* I felt the pressure of the shoot as soon as it was over, but in the middle of it, I didn't think about the fact that they were the biggest rock and roll band in the world. Some of the photographs were taken in Mexico City in 1995, in New Jersey, in Montreal, Canada and at Soldiers Field in Chicago during the opening gig in 1997.

In January of 1995, just four days before the *Stones'* first concert in Mexico City, I received a phone call from Virgin Records in Mexico asking me to go on location for the shooting of the video "I Go Wild," from the *"Voodoo Lounge"* album. The location was very different from any other location in the world—the former temple of Saint Lazarus, a seventeenth-century church. There was a kind of magic atmosphere. It

Fernando
A C E V E S

was funny to see the *Rolling Stones* in a fusion with that old building, as if they belonged to each other. At that time I had a chance to catch some images behind the scenes. I only had two minutes, so it all happened very quickly. In my first encounter with Mick Jagger, he was sitting, looking at me very fast, at my camera and what kind of equipment I was working with. After forty years of being photographed, these people know what they want from a photographer. As a photographer, you don't need to talk to them. They know what they want to show to the audience. They are the directors of themselves.

Photographing the *Stones* was a truly exciting experience. They know each other very well. I understood that for the *Rolling Stones,* playing music was as natural as walking or smiling. I didn't feel any tension, they were just playing from the soul.

As a rock and roll photographer you have to be aware of what you are doing. You have to be conscious that you are making history with your camera. The thing is just to be cool...and excited. You have to be conscious that the highest point for every rock and roll photographer is to shoot the *Rolling Stones.* There's nothing else in the world after shooting the *Stones.*

1995, KEITH RICHARDS
AND MICK JAGGER. "I GO WILD."
MEXICO CITY

1998, MICK JAGGER AND
KEITH RICHARDS. FORO SOL.
MEXICO CITY

1995, THE ROLLING STONES,
SAINT LAZARUS CHURCH, MEXICO CITY

COLOPHON

ROLLING STONES 40X20 was produced by Insight Editions
www.insighteditions.com

Chris Murray, *EDITOR*
Gordon Goff, *DIRECTOR OF SALES AND MARKETING*
Raoul Goff, *PRODUCTION DIRECTOR*
Ian Szymkowiak, *DESIGNER*
Alan Hebel & Chris Bryant, *LAYOUT AND PRODUCTION ASSOCIATES*

With special thanks to the staff at Govinda Gallery.

The text typeface is Monoco and the display faces are
Ruffian and Raw.

The text stock is 140 gsm Japanese matte art paper and printed
four color with spot gloss varnish.

This book was printed and bound by Palace Press International,
Hong Kong, under the supervision of Erik Ko.
www.palacepress.com